PAIDEIA EDUCATION

CHARLES DICKENS

Oliver Twist

Literary analysis

Paideia Education

© Paideia Education, 2020.

ISBN 978-2-7593-0699-2

Legal Deposit: september 2020

Printing Books on Demand GmbH

In de Tarpen 42

22848 Norderstedt, Germany

CONTENTS

AUTHOR'S
BIOGRAPHY

Charles Dickens was an English novelist born in Lamport, a district of Portsmouth, in 1812. Son of a modest navy treasurer and the second of eight children, Dickens lived a very hard childhood. The need for money made him leave school and work, at the age of twelve, as a hand sticking labels in a polish factory while his father was imprisoned for debt. The misery and the humiliating memory of those times obsessed him his whole life, giving him an endless theme to use in his future work, just as his being permanently in touch with the poorest areas of London has supplied his most poignant depictions.

In 1857, Dickens worked as a clerk. He learned shorthand writing, and became a court-reporter for the Parliament in 1831. At that same period, he fell in love with Maria Beadnell who was the daughter of a bank manager, but she rejected him because of his lack of money. Deeply saddened, Dickens tried to improve his situation. He became a journalist and later a columnist, and published his first book, *Sketches by Boz*, in 1835. In 1836, he married Catherine Hogarth but they were never happy. In 1857, he wrote to Collins: "This domestic unhappiness remains so strong upon me that I can't write."

The success of his *Sketches* triggered the order of a second book: *The Pickwick Papers*, published in 1837. From then on, his works followed one another, reflecting the traumas of his childhood. In *Oliver Twist*, subtitled *The Parish Boy's Progress* (1837-1838), he denounced the workhouses which enslaved the poor since the 1834 law. In *Nicholas Nickleby* (1838-1839), he criticized the industry of the soup-sellers in Yorkshire schools. In *The Old Curiosity Shop* (1840-1841), he blamed the social perversion of the capitalistic system of the time. Dickens' works have been very positively welcomed and made him one of the best-known novelists in the world.

In January 1840, he traveled to the United States but that

journey proved a bitter disappointment. The author had hoped to find democracy there, but he only managed to find a cupid, awfully conformist and slave driver society. When he went back, he published his thoughts in *American Notes for General Circulation* (1842) and in *Martin Chuzzlewit* (1843-1844). Depression was creeping in but it did not hinder his literary production. He published *A Christmas Carol* in 1843, *The Chimes* and *The Cricket on the Hearth* in 1845 while he was traveling to Italy and visiting Paris. In 1846, he founded a newspaper: *The Daily News*; and then wrote *Dombey and Son*, published in 1848.

Dickens remained obsessed by his childhood, but the vivid and painful memories stopped him from writing his autobiography. He would rather disguise the overwhelming reality of his past in *David Copperfield* (1848-1849). The theme of the miserable childhood was far from drying out: he wrote *Bleak House* (1852), *Hard Times* (1854) and *Little Dorrit* (1857-1858). In 1858, Dickens left his wife for the young actress Ellen Ternan. This new love, hardly reciprocal, affected him enormously and inspired him two novels expressing disenchantment: *Great Expectations* (1861) and *Our Mutual Friend* (1864-1865). He left *The Mystery of Edwin Drood* unfinished when he died of exhaustion in Glad's Hill Place, in 1870. The structure of his novels is quite disturbing, they proceed by successive expansions, in the plot as well as in regard to the characters who appear more and more numerous. Charles Dickens managed to move a whole generation, to make people laugh and cry by creating a world where life is abounding.

WORK
PRESENTATION

Oliver Twist, written by Charles Dickens, was first published as a monthly serial in *Bentley's Miscellany* from February 1837 to March 1839; it was the magazine for which the author had just been appointed editor-in-chief. For the first time in an English novel, the child is at the foreground, allowing Dickens to give a new vision of what life is in London's slums during the Victorian era. He does not hesitate to criticize the English society – in the middle of the industrial revolution at the time – by destroying the false image of the delinquents' world given by other novelists; Dickens thus shows a dark representation of crime and criminals.

Oliver Twist, the orphan, escapes from a workhouse where labor is hard and food lacking. Once he arrives in London, he becomes acquainted with a boy who leads him to a group of robbers controlled by Fagin, the Jew. In this communal slum, everyone tries to make a thief out of the new recruit, but the poor child irrevocably hates crime and refuses to let them pervert him. Oliver is then dragged in a series of criminal adventures and put in the hands of vile characters who will try everything to teach him the the secrets of the profession. Abandoned and exposed very early to this ruthless world, the boy miraculously manages to remain innocent. He meets people who will help him escape from the criminal slums of London and discover the secret behind his birth.

In this novel – one of Dickens' best-know work – the author explores with originality and truthful realism a very popular theme: crime. His descriptions of the London slums are particularly mind-blowing, and the depictions he makes of criminals are incredibly vivid. The adventures of the little orphan have met a considerable success.

SUMMARY

Chapter I

Oliver is born in a workhouse in England, his date of birth is deemed irrelevant. His mother asks to take a good look at him before she dies in that same place.

Chapter II

Oliver is put under the care and authority of Mrs. Mann, a nurse who has a habit of brutalizing the children she is in charge of. Mr. Bumble, the verger, comes to take Oliver to a workhouse when he becomes too old to stay at the nurse's. The mortality rate is very high at the workhouse where the residents are underfed. One day, after drawing lots, Oliver has to go and ask the supervisor for extra food. He does so, and is immediately locked up. The workhouse puts up some posters saying that 5 pounds will be offered to anyone wishing to take Oliver as an apprentice.

Chapter III

Mr. Ganfield, a chimney sweeper, sees the poster of the parish and asks for Oliver to become his trainee. To make this a valid decision, Oliver must appear before a magistrate. However, the child is unable to hold back his tears in front of the authorities, and the magistrates refuse to sign the contract. He is taken back to the workhouse.

Chapter IV

Mr. Sowerberry, the funeral director, is allowed to take Oliver as his apprentice. He becomes a handyman, and spends his first night among the coffins.

Chapter V

He is awakened by Noah Claypole, an assisted child, who hates Oliver right from the start. Mr. Sowerberry, on the contrary, likes Oliver and wants to make him an undertaker. The boy accompanies him at the burials and witnesses miserable scenes.

Chapter VI

Oliver officially becomes an apprentice. But Noah, Charlotte – a young sloven girl – and Mrs. Sowerberry are his enemies. One day, Noah comes to insult Oliver's mother. The boy then bursts out of his passivity and becomes so enraged that he is locked up in the cellar.

Chapter VII

Noah runs to Mr. Bumble at the workhouse and assures him Oliver has tried to kill him. The boy takes a beating and remains locked up. But the next morning he escapes and, while walking past the workhouse, he sees his old friend, Dick, who tells him that he is going to die.

Chapter VIII

Oliver decides to walk to London. After a week he arrives to Barnet, a city where he meets a boy of his age but looking like a man. It is Jack Dawkins, nicknamed "The Artful Dodger". He leads Oliver to London where he knows a man who can offer him hospitality. Oliver finds himself in a dark house inhabited by Mr. Fagin – the old Jew – and a group of youngsters.

Chapter IX

Oliver, supposed to be asleep, gets a glimpse of the Jew taking his fortune out of a trapdoor. The Dodger arrives with Charley Bates, one of his comrades, and they show Fagin their loot. Oliver does not understand that he is in a den of thieves. Then, he meets Bet and Nancy, two girls who also conduct business with the Jew.

Chapter X

Oliver goes out with the Dodger and Charley Bates for the first time. The both of them steal a man's handkerchief in front of a bookstore. Horrified, Oliver runs, so the man assumes that he is guilty and starts chasing him. Soon, a whole crowd is after him. Oliver falls, the robbed man takes pity on him but a police officer arrests him.

Chapter XI

Oliver appears before a magistrate. The robbed man, Mr. Brownlow thinks that Oliver may not be guilty. But the magistrate, Mr. Fang, sentences him to three months of forced labor before the bookseller, who saw it all happen, arrives to restore the truth: it was two other youths who committed the crime. Oliver, who passed out during the session, has his case dismissed. Mr. Brownlow takes him under his wing and brings him to his sumptuous mansion to tend to his health.

Chapter XII

Oliver, very weakened, almost dies. An old lady, Mrs. Bedwin, looks after him during his recovery. A painting in the mansion catches Oliver's eye; it is the picture of a woman with a sad look. Mr. Brownlow is intrigued by the resemblance between the portrait and the boy. Then the narrator tells how The Dodger and Charley Bates went back at the Jew's after the theft and informed him of Oliver's troubles with the law.

Chapter XIII

Bill Sikes, a 35-year-old ruffian, arrives at Fagin's with his white dog. They argue to know who will go and seek information about Oliver at the police. It is Nancy who goes there posing as Oliver's sister. An officer tells her that he was taken by a man.

Chapter XIV

Oliver lives the happiest days of his life. Mr. Brownlow asks him to tell him about his story when Mr. Grimwig, an old man, interrupts them. Mr. Brownlow then sends Oliver to bring back some books to the bookstore. Mr. Grimwig, doubting Oliver, assures that the boy will jump at the chance to flee with the books and never come back.

Chapter XV

Nancy stumbles on Oliver while he is going to the bookstore and, claiming he is her brother, kidnaps him with the help of Sikes.

Chapter XVI

Oliver is at the Jew's place again, he tries to escape. Fagin hits him but Nancy stands up for him. A violent argument between Nancy, Fagin and Sikes follows.

Chapter XVII

Meanwhile, at the workhouse, Mr. Bumble pays a visit to Mrs. Mann. They talk about a boy considered ill-tempered: it is the young Dick, Oliver's dying friend. The boy is asking to leave a message of affection to Oliver before dying. Both the adults are outraged.

Mr. Bumble goes to London for business, and discovers in the newspaper that Mr. Brownlow is looking for Oliver and offers a reward to any person with information about him. So the verger goes to Mr. Brownlow's mansion and makes a scoundrel of Oliver. From then on, Mr. Brownlow does not want to hear about the boy anymore.

Chapter XVIII

Fagin locks up Oliver in the house, so that he knows what loneliness is. Thus the boy begins to appreciate company, even that of Fagin and those under his care. However, he still refuses to become a thief. Tom Chilting, an 18-year-old man whom Oliver has never seen before, pays a visit to Fagin.

Chapter XIX

Fagin arrives at Sikes and Nancy's place to talk business. They speak about a burglary that Sikes and a certain Toby Crackit are to perpetrate. But they need a small child to give them a hand: it will be Oliver.

Chapter XX

On the next day, Nancy unwillingly comes to fetch and take Oliver to Sikes. The latter informs the boy that at the slightest misbehavior he will be shot dead. Oliver stays at Sikes' for the night and wakes up at 5 the next morning to go on the expedition.

Chapter XXI

Oliver and Sikes walk all day long, then they stop at an inn for the night. The next day, a peasant takes them to Shepperton in coach. There, they enter an uninhabited house.

Chapter XXII

In the house, they find Toby Crackit. They go to Chertsey during the night, and climb over the wall of the house they are going to rob. Oliver's task is to enter the house through a small window, so that he can later open the door to the two burglars. But the domestic staff hear some noise and shoot at Oliver. So the thieves take the boy with them and flee.

Chapter XXIII

Mrs. Corney, the manager of the workhouse where Oliver was born, receives a visit from Mr. Bumble. A quite ridiculous scene of seduction between the two characters follows, until a wretched girl informs Mrs. Corney that an old woman named Sally is dying and wishes to talk to her.

Chapter XXIV

The old Sally is no other than the woman who assisted Oliver's mother while she gave birth to him. She tells Mrs. Corney that she has stolen the belongings of the boy's mother. Yet these objects should have been given to Oliver and would have helped him to find where he is from.

Chapter XXV

Toby Crackit arrives at Fagin's den to inform him that the burglary failed and that the two thieves have been forced to leave Oliver in a ditch when they were chased by the domestic staff. As for Sikes, his location remains unknown.

Chapter XXVI

Fagin goes to "The Three Cripples", the inn where he usually meets with Sikes. He is looking for a man named Monks but he is not there. So he goes to Nancy's in order to ask her if she knows where Sikes might be. The woman does not know anything. When he goes back to his place, Monks is waiting for him. We learn that Monks has been looking for Oliver for years, but we still ignore why.

Chapter XXVII

After the revelations of the dying woman, Mrs. Corney goes back home. Mr. Bumble is still there and proposes to her. She says yes. The man then goes to Mr. Sowerberry's place and scolds Noah Claypole who was kissing Charlotte.

Chapter XXVIII

Oliver has spent the night in the ditch where Sikes had left him. He regains consciousness and discovers that his left arm is wounded. He goes back to the burglary scene to ask for help to the very persons who shot him. Mr. Giles, the butler, takes Oliver in though he is still glad to have wounded the young villain the night before.

Chapter XXIX

Doctor Losberne is called to heal Oliver. The lady of the house, Mrs. Maylie, and her niece, Rose Maylie, refuse to see the injured boy. Mr. Losberne invites them to do so, as they imagine the villain to be a grown up man.

Chapter XXX

The two ladies become aware that the thief is just a poor boy. They ask Oliver to tell them his story, and are deeply moved by the account. So, with the doctor, they decide to help him. Then Mr. Losberne tries to prove to Mr. Giles that the person he shot the day before might as well be someone else. Mr. Giles begins to doubt, but the rest of the domestic staff has already sent for police sergeants in order to solve the case.

Chapter XXXI

Mr. Losberne tells the sergeants – Blathers and Duff – that Oliver was wounded by a trap while playing in a park. As for Mr. Giles, he is unable to tell if the boy in front of him is really the one he shot or not.

Chapter XXXII

Oliver lives a happy life with Rose and Mrs. Maylie. To please him, M. Losberne takes him to his former benefactor: Mr. Brownlow. But the latter left for the West Indies. Then, the Maylies go to the countryside with Oliver. Thus, three months of happiness flow by.

Chapter XXXIII

However, Rose falls gravely ill. Oliver must go to the city to have a letter delivered to Doctor Losberne. On his way back, he bumps into a man who starts insulting him, and passes out. The staff of an inn takes care of him. When he goes back, Oliver learns that Rose is cured.

Chapter XXXIV

Harry Maylie, Mrs. Maylie's son, alerted by letter of Rose's illness, arrives at his mother's. He learns that the young lady is cured. Harry speaks with his mother and tells her about the feelings he has been having for Rose for so long. But Mrs. Maylie has always disapproved of this union because of the mystery around her niece's birth. She fears that one day, he is going to leave her.

One night, Oliver rests near the window where he usually studies, and looking up, he sees the Jew and the man who insulted him several days earlier in front of the inn – who is no other than Monks. They are looking at him from the yard.

Chapter XXXV

Harry Maylie and Mr. Losberne look in vain for the two

intruders. After a while, the incident is forgotten. Harry once again declares his love for Rose, but she refuses to plan a future with him; she is afraid of jeopardizing her future life because of the dubious circumstances of her birth. Harry makes her the promise of seeing her again after one year, so that he can try one last time to make her change her mind about him.

Chapter XXXVI

Mr. Losberne and Harry are about to leave. Harry asks Oliver to write him a letter every fortnight to tell him about Rose and her feelings. The girl who deep inside is in love with Harry, watches his departure crying.

Chapter XXXVII

Mr. Bumble is no longer a verger, but became the chief warden of the workhouse. He does not love his wife anymore, and she does not hesitate to hit him when he gets obnoxious with her or to humiliate him in front of the paupers.

He enters the inn where Monks is. And Monks was precisely looking for him, he wants information about Oliver. Mr. Bumble who intends to squeeze money out of him, assures him that his wife is the last person to have spoken with the midwife who brought Oliver to this world. Mrs. Corney will come and tell him what she knows on the next day.

Chapter XXXVIII

Mr. Bumble and Mrs. Corney go to the meeting, in a tumbledown building. In exchange for 25 pounds, Mrs. Corney explains that the old Sally has stolen from Oliver's mother a necklace and a wedding ring engraved with the name

"Agnes". Monks, after taking back these belongings, opens a trapdoor just above the river, and drops the jewelry in the water. There is no longer any real evidence of Oliver's true identity.

Chapter XXXIX

Sikes fell ill, and is taken care of by Nancy who lives with him in extreme poverty. Fagin pays him a visit and has Nancy leave with him so that she can bring back some money after the Jew gives her some. But Monks arrives when Fagin and Nancy are at the thieves' den. She can't help but listening to their conversation and she is quite shocked. When she gets back at Sikes', she gives him a sleeping pill and goes to look for Rose in order to reveal everything the two men said.

Chapter XL

Rose gently welcomes Nancy, which moves her. Nancy tells her that Monks is in fact Oliver's brother and that he has ruled him out of the inheritance by throwing the evidence of his origins into the river. He has also put Fagin in charge of finding and bringing Oliver back to him. Nancy plans to meet Rose every Sunday night between 11p.m and midnight on the London Bridge. Rose wants to help Nancy change her life, but she refuses out of love for Sikes even though he abuses her.

Chapter XLI

Oliver informs Rose that Mr. Brownlow is back from his trip. They both go to Oliver's benefactor's place. Rose proceeds to tell him about the boy's adventures and so restores the image he had of him. She also reveals the secret Nancy told her. A meeting takes place between Mr. Brownlow, Rose, Mrs. Maylie and Mr. Losberne. They decide to find the truth about Oliver's identity and to give him back the inheritance of which he was deprived. Harry and Mr. Grimwig will help them.

Chapter XLII

Noah and Charlotte escaped from Mr. Sowerberry's after stealing all the money from the cash register. They stop at "The Three Cripples" for the night. Fagin, who overhears Noah saying that he would like to become a thief, comes and asks him to join his group. They plan a meeting for the next day. Noah is now called Morris Bolter.

Chapter XLIII

Fagin speaks with Noah and tells him that his best recruit has been arrested: it is The Dodger. Charley Bates enters and informs Fagin that The Dodger's case is hopeless. Noah is put in charge of going to the prison and figure out how this will end. The Dodger is after all sent back to court.

Chapter XLIV

Nancy tries to make it to her meeting with Rose but Sikes locks the door, beats her and forbids her to go out. Fagin, who witnesses the scene, thinks Nancy is in love with someone else. He jumps on this chance to subtly suggest her to take revenge on Sikes. Because the Jew secretly dreams of poisoning Sikes whom he hates. But Nancy refuses to deal with him.

Chapter XLV

On the next day, Fagin asks Noah to tail Nancy. He must do it on the next Sunday.

Chapter XLVI

Noah follows Nancy to the London Bridge where she meets with Rose and Mr. Brownlow. The man asks Nancy to give him a portrait of Monks so that he can find him. According to Nancy's depiction, Brownlow thinks he knows the man. Nancy refuses one last time to live a better life and goes back to Sikes.

Chapter XLVII

Fagin tells Sikes that Nancy betrayed them. So Sikes goes back to her and kills her, beating her with a bludgeon.

Chapter XLVIII

Sikes leaves his house and wanders in the streets. He notes that the news of the murder he committed has already spread in town. He finds himself a place for the night but the image of Nancy's corpse haunts him. He sees a fire quite far away and decides to go and help the people put it out in order to forget his atrocious deed. Then he decides to go back to London, thinking the authorities would not be looking for him there. He tries to drown his dog so that people will not recognize his description but it understands its owner's thoughts and flees.

Chapter XLIX

Mr. Brownlow manages to capture Monks and brings him home. Monks' real name is Edward Leeford and he is the son of one of Mr. Brownlow's late friend: Edwin Leeford. Edwin left Edward's mother when he was a child and settled in England where he met Agnes, Oliver's mother. Edwin died during a journey in Rome and Agnes died after giving birth to Edwin Leeford's illegitimate child. Then Monks inherited from his father because his mother had destroyed the will which included Oliver. Monks is forced to sign the statement he just made because Mr. Brownlow threatens to call the police if he does not cooperate.

Chapter L

Toby Crackit, Mr. Chilting and an escaped convict found refuge in an abandoned house on Jacob Island. We learn that Fagin has been arrested by the police. Sikes arrives to the house preceded by his dog. Charles Bates enters too and, seeing Sikes, he can't help but hitting him and calling him a murderer. But the house is soon surrounded both by police officers and inhabitants. Sikes tries to escape through the roof with a rope, but loses his balance and ends up hanged to this very rope. As for his dog, it tries to jump on its master's shoulders but it falls into the ditch and dies.

Chapter LI

Oliver and his friends go back to his hometown. Mr. Brownlow forces Monks to repeat his confession in person, in Mr. Bumble and his wife's presence in order to confirm what he says. We also learn that Rose is no other than Agnes' sister, and therefore, Oliver's aunt. Her father died when she was a child and Mrs. Maylie who took her in. It is Monks' mother who started the rumor that she was the illegitimate daughter of crazy people. Harry Maylie arrives right in the middle of this revelation; he became a clergyman and gave up on his big career out of love for Rose. He proposes to her and she says yes.

Chapter LII

Fagin is sentenced to death and awaits his punishment in a cell. Mr. Brownlow and Oliver visit him. They want the papers given to him by Monks about Oliver's inheritance. Fagin discloses his hiding place to the boy.

Chapter LIII

Rose is now married to Harry, Mrs. Maylie lives close by, as well as Mr. Losberne and Mr. Brownlow who finally adopted Oliver. Monks who received, thanks to Mr. Brownlow's kindness, half of Oliver's inheritance went and started over, but he fell into his old habits again and ended up dying in jail. Noah Claypole became a professional snitch. Mr. and Mrs Bumble were deprived of their situation because of their dealings and became residents of the workhouse they once were the masters of. As for Charley Bates, he decided to live an honest life.

REASONS
OF SUCCESS

During the Victorian Era (1837-1901), literature evolved with the social relations and habits. Few English writers operated the transition between romanticism and Victorian novel, like Balzac or Stendhal did in France. Nevertheless, the Brontë sisters who dominated the first half of the century and made way for the Victorian novels – while reconciling both romanticism and Gothic novel, their works address modern themes and foreshadow a critical realism – had a notable influence. Romanticism progressively gave way to realism, and a lot of great quality works started to show. The Victorian Era is considered in many regards as the most prolific period for British novels: serial novels and popular novels triumph.

Dickens' work greatly contributed to this evolution in literature. His part in Victorian England is immense: not only does he show one of the most vivid and realistic representations of 19th century England in the middle of the industrial revolution, but he also creates impressive characters. With *Oliver Twist*, Dickens describes criminal characters very credibly and convincingly (especially Fagin, the Jew, who is one of the most unforgettable characters of British literature), and the hero is an innocent child who falls into the hands of villains. By placing a poor child right in the middle of violence, prostitution, delinquency and crime, Dickens only enforces his criticism of banditry and urban insecurity.

During the Victorian period, crime was a big subject of concern, the Newgate novels, depicting criminals sympathetically, had become very popular since the publication of *Paul Clifford*, by Edward Bulwer-Lytton, in 1830. This very controversial genre was none the less extremely popular and aroused an unprecedented impact upon the Victorian reader. Dickens, however, wanted his novel to be different than the other Newgate novels which, according to him, were too idealizing and made the criminal's life too attractive. Instead

37

of depicting charming and elegant bandits and of showing the villain's life as a sort of thrilling adventure, the author takes us into the dark slums of London with an originality and a realistic truth of the most striking kind.

Dickens' style, mixing humor and pathos, constitutes an effective weapon aiming to denounce misery, cruelty, crime, urban insecurity, corruption and child exploitation. The author shows us, through a child's eye, what life is like at the lower rungs of the Victorian society. He is interested in all the matters of his time, without actually angering the readers or offending the norms of the Victorian period with too brutal or violent approaches. Keen reader of the "sentimental" writers of the 18th century, Dickens does not hesitate to use the pathos in order to move and make his readers laugh through touching emotions and feelings. Therefore, he gladly modifies the behavior or fate of his characters according to the readers' reaction, which he can anticipate thanks to the monthly serial publication of the novel.

Oliver Twist met a considerable success. From this striking picture of London's criminal slums emerges a realism which will, in turn, deeply influence the works of famous writers such as Anne Rice, Dostoyevsky, Thomas Hardy and many others.

MAIN
THEMES

With *Oliver Twist*, Dickens exploits the theme of criminality. By taking an innocent orphan child who falls into the hands of a group of villains as main character, the author shows how crime is born as well as a panorama of bandits and banditry during the Victorian Era.

How does Dickens manage to represent crime and criminals while, at the time, crime was considered the worst offense? His main motive, as he points out in the new 1841 preface, is to show how bandits really live in order to dissuade the poor from turning towards this way of life – in this regard, his novel is different from the other Newgate novels which, according to him, are too idealizing and represent a delinquent's life as an amusing adventure: "It appeared to me that to draw a knot of such associates in crime as really do exist, to paint them in all their deformity, in all their wretchedness, in all the squalid poverty of their lives […] would be an attempt at something […] which would be a service to society." Dickens wants to show that living with a group of villains has nothing to be delighted about, he thus paints crime and criminals in the heart of London, in the middle of the industrial revolution, with precision, originality and realistic truth.

In every novel, starting from *Paul Clifford* by Edward Bulwer-Lytton, Bandits are charming and attractive. Dickens, on the contrary, does not try to make his criminal characters elegant. Depicted very credibly and truthfully, they rather inspire horror and disgust: "[…] none of the attractions of dress, no embroidery, no lace, no jack-boots, no crimson coats and ruffles", says Dickens in his preface. Moreover, Fagin, the chief of the young crime associates, is dressed in a fustian. Right at his first appearance in the novel, he is described as "a very old shriveled Jew, whose villainous-looking and repulsive face was obscured by a quantity of matted red hair" and wears "a greasy flannel gown, with his throat bare."

In Dickens' novel, the use of the word "engaging", when referring to criminals, has a clear ironic connotation. Thus, the author speaks of an "engaging ruffian" just after the satirical depiction of Bill Sikes who is dressed in dirty gray cotton clothes and has a "broad heavy countenance with a beard of three days' growth, and two scowling eyes." The physical description of this evildoer is even more precise and repellent than that of Fagin and reveals right from the start the indifferent and cruel nature of the character the deep cruelty of whom seems absolutely incurable. In this regard, the evil characters of the novel detach themselves from those in all the previous criminal stories, through the richness of their personalities, their repulsive looks and the harsh reality of their bandit life.

Even concerning the very criminal act, Dickens gives a detailed and terrifying picture: "It was a ghastly figure to look upon," he says about Nancy's murder by Sikes. The author points out the "foulest and most cruel" of horrors when the sunlight enters the room where lies the prostitute's corpse with, on the ceiling, "the reflection of the pool of gore that quivered and danced."

Crime and criminals are therefore described by Dickens with a nuanced realism, reflecting the brutal truth of the city's criminal slums. Villains are everything but engaging, and the daily life of the bandit is far from being a thrilling adventure. Besides, for most of the characters, this criminal life is not a choice: Dickens wants to show how young children can become evil when they are left alone in the corrupted world that is a city in the process of industrialization.

But what, for Dickens, generates a criminal behavior? With *Oliver Twist*, the author wants to show that the Victorian perspective on crime is wrong. Indeed, at the time, the poor were considered to be criminals from the moment they were born and destined by their birth to disturb the public order. Yet, according to Dickens, crime is no legacy. It is external influences which are really the cause for criminal behavior, rather than a naturally vicious personality. Thus, the influence of suspicious people like Fagin, and mostly the hostile environment (London's slums) are, to him, the heart of deviance, the primary origin of crime.

In Dickens' work, London, going through the industrial revolution, appears as a filthy, miserable and gloomy maze, which brings about wandering, loss and wretchedness. The urban disorder is particularly visible when the furious crowd is chasing after Oliver who has been wrongly accused of having stolen Mr. Brownlow's handkerchief: "Away they run, pell-mell, helter-skelter, slap-dash [...] and streets, squares, and courts, reecho with the sound." The winding streets are dark and narrow, and the characters move or lose themselves in a maze of filth and misery.

To describe the moribund and unfriendly atmosphere of the city, Dickens sometimes resorts to a gloomy fantastic instead of realism, especially when the old Fagin is headed towards Spitalfields: "The mud lay thick upon the stones, and a black mist hung over the streets ; the rain fell sluggishly down, and everything felt cold and clammy to the touch." From this fantastic place loom repulsive and horrific creatures: "The hideous old man [Fagin] seemed like some loathsome reptile, engendered in the slime and darkness through which he moved : crawling forth, by night, in search of some rich offal for a meal." Dickens thus criticizes the urban insecurity and a city full of monsters where life is often nothing more than a struggle for survival.

In this corrupted and damaged world, among all these dubious people leading lives of bandits, thieves or prostitutes, the author places Oliver Twist, a poor child pure in heart. This orphan by birth escapes a workhouse where labor is hard and food lacking, and quickly finds himself taken into the criminal slums of the city. How does the child manages to stay innocent in this ruthless world? Can he resist evil and crime, the only alternatives he seems to have?

Oliver Twist is described as a naive, thin and puny child, victim of the adults' negligence and of his ignorance of London's streets. When he arrives in the city, after escaping the workhouse, he is famished, exhausted and desperate. This is when he meets a strange boy, Jack Dawkins, who will take him to a group of outlaws under the authority of the old Fagin, a Jewish receiver of stolen goods. In fact, Fagin recruits lonely and desperate children in order to make bandits out of them, and this perversion process is usually successful: Charley Bates, Jack Dawkins, the Artful Dodger, and many more got the basics of the profession from him, and became experienced thieves. If not fundamentally evil, they nevertheless appear easily corruptible. Charley Bates, for instance, does not hesitate to laugh "uproariously" to Fagin's jokes.

In this communal slum, they try to pervert Oliver, to make him a novice thief. Little by little, he is taught the rules of the profession, but the boy shows an unwavering hatred for theft. Conversely to his comrades, it seems he can't be forced to do chores and his deep naivety miraculously keeps him from bad influences: "Oh! Pray have mercy on me, and do not make me steal," he begs. Fagin is also startled by Oliver's resistance to vice: "I had no hold upon him to make him worse […]. His hand was not in. I had nothing to frighten him with." For some time, Oliver escapes his sinister companions, but he is quickly taken back by the group and delivered to the dreadful Sikes who continues his instruction as novice thief; in vain, because the bandits can't get anything from him, except by using fear: "Say another word, and I'll do your business myself with a crack on the head," says Sikes just before an attempted burglary. In spite of this tumultuous life, Oliver knows how to stay away from the criminal's influence and remains innocent. This way, Dickens wants to show that when a man's nature is essentially good, it can overlook the most cruel experiences without giving in to crime.

The treatment inflicted to the main characters is a crucial step in the Newgate novels. How does Dickens choose to punish the villains? Fagin is arrested and sentenced to death. Monks dies in prison. But most of the time, the author would rather punish the criminals himself through some unexpected accidents instead of throwing them in jail where they would be delivered to the executioner. The sudden end of Bill Sikes is undoubtedly the most spectacular death of the novel: he hangs himself by accident while jumping off the roof of a building in order to escape his pursuers. As for Mr. and Mrs Bumble, they are deprived of their situation because of their dealings, and become the residents of the workhouse they once were the masters of. However, the corrupted children, because they were left into an awful environment, are usually shown mercy: Noah Claypole, the coward, becomes a professional snitch, Charley Bates, decides to lead an honest life.

ANALYSIS OF THE
LITERARY MOVEMENT

Oliver Twist is part of a literary movement where novels, taking an objective vision of the world as a rule, pretend to represent nature and life as they really are: it is realism. The word appears in *The Mercure de France*, in 1829, and then in *The Revue des deux Mondes* (Review of the Two Worlds), in 1834. Realism, in the broad sense of the word, has always been present in the literary life, from the Homeric poem to Molière's comedy. But it is particularly attributed to a precise moment in literature, between 1850 and 1890.

In France, the June Days Uprising in 1848 and the coup of Louis-Napoleon provoked a reaction in literature: the failed revolutions mark the end of many Romantic hopes. The readers are weary of the sentimental effusions, and the great masters of Romanticism cease to write or publish poetry. This is when realism appears in literature, as a reaction to the lyrical outpourings and excessive imagination of the Romantic movement. But it is in the "representation" of reality and not in its "reproduction" that the 19th century innovates (there is already a certain kind of realism in the works of great authors of the 18th century like Marivaux, Prévost or Restif de la Bretonne). The authors try to represent the most mundane reality with an objectivity unadorned by verses or imagination, and two novelists become, despite themselves, the pioneers of the movement: Stendhal and Balzac who, romanticists in certain aspects, are also realists in others. *The Red and The Black*, 1830, inspired of a real news item and showing different points of view, opens the way for the "realist" writers. In *The Human Comedy* (1830-1856), Balzac meticulously describes the habits of his time and almost scientifically analyzes man. But it is with Flaubert, in spite of his refusal to be part of a school, that realism reaches its zenith with the disillusion of the main character in *Sentimental Education* (1869), or the representation of a dull and boring life in *Madame Bovary* (1856).

This response to the excesses of Romanticism is not limited to France, even if it is where it was the most clearly asserted (especially thanks to Champfleury who became, despite himself, the theorist of realism since his preface in 1847 to a book entitled *Le Réalisme*). The manifestations of realism in other countries, mostly due to the French influence, triggers the emergence of great names in the literary history: in the United States, Herman Melville, Harriet-Beecher Stowe, Louisa May Alcott, Jack London and Bret Harte are the most remarkable representatives of the realist movement. In Russia, Leon Tolstoy, Fyodor Dostoyevsky. In England, Charles Dickens appears as the great master of the social novel.

To the lyrical excesses of Romanticism, he opposes the scientific analyzes, the precise study of events, species and environments. In his quest for a scientific truth, and to represent reality in the most objective manner, with no ornaments or idealization, Dickens applies methods taken from experimental sciences and philosophical positivism. He frees himself from the elevated language and takes interest in the middle or popular classes in dealing with misery, domestic relations, the influence of their environment on people, the mediocrity of their daily lives, the social ladder, etc...

Realism, a reaction of sensitivity more than a movement, is a phase of transition in the literary history. Champfleury wrote, as early as 1857: "The word realism, a word of transition which won't last more than three decades..." Around 1880, the movement evolves towards naturalism, the literary aesthetics of which are defined by Emile Zola. Naturalism is in charge of fulfilling what realism had started, by pushing the strictness of reality in the novels even further.